ADAGIO

poems by

Lana Bella

Finishing Line Press
Georgetown, Kentucky

ADAGIO

Copyright © 2017 by Lana Bella
ISBN 978-1-63534-084-6 First Edition
All rights reserved under International and Pan-American Copyright Conventions. No part of this book may be reproduced in any manner whatsoever without written permission from the publisher, except in the case of brief quotations embodied in critical articles and reviews.

ACKNOWLEDGMENTS

ADAGIO, *Fish Food Magazine*
THE HALVED NOTES, *Chiron Review*
THIS IS EVERY LOVE STORY EVER TOLD, *Riding Light Magazine*
A NIGHT IN HARLEM, *Bewildering Stories*
THE HOUSE OF WRINKLED BONES, *Literary Orphans*
FINGERS ON THE PIANO KEYS, *Quail Bell Magazine*
LUC, *Mothers Always Write* (NOMINATED FOR THE PUSHCART PRIZE)
UPTURNED HAND, *The Criterion Journal*
THE ELUSIVE MERMAID, *QLRS* (SINGAPORE)
DOPPELGANGER, *Of Zoos Magazine* (SINGAPORE)
A KNITTED DAY, *The Corner Club Press*
UNIVERSAL CARVING, *Unlikely Stories*
GRAPHIC NOVEL, *Poetry Salzburg Review*
CONSENT TO NOTHING AND YOURSELF UNSEEING, *Indiana Voice Journal*
SYNCHRONICITY, *Literary Orphans*
SMALL AND SMALLER, *Coe Review*
RU, *Poetry Salzburg Review*
THERE IS A CRACK IN EVERYTHING, *Unbroken Journal*
THE LEAVING GIRL, *Chantarelle's Notebook*
MIGRAINE, *Subterranean Poetry*
THE CASUALTY OF A FORGOTTEN BOOK, *Marco Polo Arts Lit*
LINGUISTIC SILENCE, *Calliope Magazine*
TIME, *Quail Bell Magazine* (FEATURED ARTIST)
A FACE IN AN ENDLESS SEA, *Poetry Quarterly*
INVISIBILITY IN WATER, *Poetry Salzburg Review*

Publisher: Leah Maines
Editor: Christen Kincaid
Cover Art: Lana Bella
Author Photo: Lana Bella
Cover Design: Elizabeth Maines

Printed in the USA on acid-free paper.
Order online: www.finishinglinepress.com
        also available on amazon.com

Author inquiries and mail orders:
Finishing Line Press
P. O. Box 1626
Georgetown, Kentucky 40324
U. S. A.

Table of Contents

Adagio, pg 1

The Halved Notes, pg 2

This is Every Love Story ever Told, pg 3

A Night in Harlem, pg 4

The House of Wrinkled Bones, pg 5

Fingers on the Piano Keys, pg 6

Luc, pg 7-8

Upturned Hand, pg 9

The Elusive Mermaid, pg 10

Doppelgänger, pg 11

A Knitted Day, pg 12

Universal Carving, pg 13

Graphic Novel, pg 14

Consent to Nothing, and Yourself Unseeing, pg 15

Synchronicity, pg 16

Small and Smaller, pg 17

Ru, pg 18

There is a Crack in Everything, pg 19

The Leaving Girl, pg 20

Migraine, pg 21

The Casualty of a Forgotten Book pg 22

Linguistics Silence, pg 23

Time, pg 24

A Face in an Endless Sea, pg 25

Invisibility in Water, pg 26

For Yuki, Malia, B.T.S., Van, Papa, Mama, Grandpa Tony, and finally, for the three and a half people who will actually give a shit to read this skimpy book of poetry.

-With gratitude, LB.

ADAGIO

There is a girl who steals away with the glow from the moon. Air churns desperately in the shadow, wingless things span across the lawn coursing beneath the enthroned adagio. She coasts her arms pulsing of fireflies, as thin hips sway against melodies unfurling in homespun cacophony, tinged with starless sky. Her dress is silent stirring the wet grass, cotton hems tease the pneumatic grip of the night soil. But like a recluse the dance is a lonely one, solitude bars witnesses to her flawless rhythms and the magic that flirts her hallowed skin. Yet, this quiet plan, though set all wrong, moves her from black to white, lets her see beyond the compass of sight: clear and omnipresent. And that sometimes she even let slip from memory that she is born blind.

THE HALVED NOTES

Just one single scratchy chirp from the bow across
the cello string, an octave spills then slides down
the tailpiece. It splits in half, one part falls on your
fingertip, the other scissors soft blue air, but always
either too much when joined, or nothing at all when
torn. If you could pluck a thousand days away with
light grounds your eyes, and a thousand nights with
darkness turns inward the bitter pith, you would tune
feverishly under a restless sun and restive moon. It
is both a necessity and luxury living within the flesh
that churns forever of music, the same way a vat of
broth seethes with rich spices. You stir the liquid but
know not when the stock is done as the arms start
to drag, and just like ripples crossing the lake, you
travel on the back of fluid folds, tucking rose-lipped
sound of the half-note where your finger wades the
water, as its twin leaps from the butterfly wings—fuse
together at the middlemost where harmony holds court.

THIS IS EVERY LOVE STORY EVER TOLD

you are a rotten tangerine hanging on
the bough of my tree, half in waiting
to splinter off, the other half already
bruised through from maturity and
hungry worms—

I watch westerly wind leaps into your
gaping rind, sunlight snakes beneath
your insides like the way ocean rushes
toward caves and dunes, leaving just
enough mystique in its wake—

seeing your whole spotted and incised,
I arch my limbs past the shingled wall
then over the ground to catch your fall,
you look at me with sad orange eyes still
wet of juice before hurling earthward in
scattering core, seeds and open pith—

someday I'll look back on this moment
and wish I'd known how to follow you
home through black, for this is you and
me born of sun, sugar and dirt, before
you stumble and fall, before I lose all
my leaves to despair—

A NIGHT IN HARLEM

Darkness dives upon Harlem,
tearing off the moon from the knife-edged snow
splinters of gold bleed the ground,
and smear the lidded heads of thick human throng.
Set bay windows stack in symmetry under the
shop awnings,
chalky flakes blur the cut-out frames,
glowing of scavenged light.
Tonight, the moon hitches on the back of sleep,
snagging flying notes ping-pong over from
the nearby Paris Blues' bar,
where a drove of patrons loiters on pulverized sidewalk,
a ghost of mist snake round their scuffed boots,
as yellow cabs scurry upon potholed street, spewing an ocean of acid rain.
A short-skirted dame tumbles out of a dark limousine
with spinning wheels by the loading dock,
a textile cloud of laurel green, champagne pink and licorice black,
struts up the steps,
trailing of perfume and sable fur.
Patting her puffed up hair,
tossing a hello at the bouncer there,
she digs through her long-strap purse for a pack
of Lucky Strike.
Cold air slaps wild and hard,
she lurches to cordon off the blast with her cupped fingers over
the cigarette, and the others flick fast on the flint wheel
it sputters then jolts to life in curious
states, part wind, part snow, part pitfall
the slim butt passes from stained lips
into deep smoky drags
entering, exiting,
then settling like a goodbye kiss as
she draws in the burned foliage of the evening,
tasting stale breath and hollow New York's moon.

THE HOUSE OF WRINKLED BONES

Outside, the air is crisp with wrinkled bones,
while the violet hours
slowly discard its poorly dressed skin
over the starved body
before slinking atop the frosty ground;
when the crescent moon
slopes saffron rays upon a lone woman
in a house gnarls of bordered evergreens.
Inside, long, white drapes
sweep the brown-carpeted floor,
as she sits by a squeaky window with its chipping paint
worn down from years of famished termites and rotting rain,
waiting there,
reeling in her foamed suspension
for the visiting ghost to
roll out of its pockmarked void at the chimes
of midnight bells.
Dung smoke knits the sleeping cold a wisp of pale sweater,
slightly puckered where the skirting tears,
when it lurks beneath the gold-crocheted chair,
that is wrought with ivory roses and cat's eye stitch,
the woman stirs.
Eyes shift, nose sniffs the flowing scent, tongue darts
to taste the turning air
then she leans out,
with clawed whisper of
cold fingertips,
reaches over to stroke
the low-hanging stumps,
smooths back the sloppy curls of its silvered mane
grasps the unfurled hands
and sways against the caressed notes of
a carved out mandolin.

FINGERS ON THE PIANO KEYS

You still miss me from the time:
I drew upon your lips with my whiskey-laced fingers;
the fingers that I'd danced across smooth
dual-toned piano keys,
to the tattooed flesh with engraved beast
on the strapping bicep.
Your breaths came through heavy and sweet
stirring gone the cigar smoke,
so close I could taste your frothy scent.
You leaned forward, both arms resting
on the console grand,
where throbbing veins ached rhythms of
the briny sea.
There, at the scarred shadow of your funny bone:
clear echo of painted ships
and pine-knot smokes,
a well-dressed suit of slate-flawed skin;
dusky light swept gold the blunt-cut fingertips,
slow whirl of the ceiling fan skimmed across
your brown hair cool.
Into the whiskey-varnished air and against
the wisps of smoldering mist,
my fingers flirted with the familiar refuge of octaves'
crunched desire and toyed sleigh bells,
upon the ivory white and charcoal black
keys of the piano.

LUC*

I remember dreaming in words of which
I could not speak, and fearing thoughts
of which I could not hold. Draped over
me like a long-tailed chill. Then I fall in
love with a boy who delivers me from the
whispering ghosts. His tight hugs are so
warm, his kisses sweet. And from the
power that be, life spills as darkness takes
to fright.

Swifter and yet more swift, the light from
which our dual skin coalesces, sloping down
upon a steep descent on my bicycle handle
bar. An alloy of spring rain-drops and winter
snow, the gold beneath the silvered white.
We become one just before the sun grows
cold and the world's envy steals our names.
Brown eyes and sooty hair, he shakes the
fallen strand where it curls into beads of
sweat. Leaps out of my hands, half in rueful
smiles, the other half in veiled consciousness.

Sometimes, this boy, of six years and four
months, who would burrow into my skin
with broken sentences and waiting space.
Then, other times, it seems as though I
could mosey on forever upon his solid para-
graphs without the need for punctuation.

My mind recalls the pockets of his tattered
cries now and again, worn into the cracks
of my heart. And the world, whose coldness
I fear will fell the green summer in his eyes.
So, I shall stay awake. In blurred delirium.
In lucid fever. In a storm of sunset rain then
sunrise drought. And I shall stay through
the surfaced joy then strangling despair.

For I know him like I know my own skin. Like
A poet knows his consonant and vowels. Like
a mother's ocean that drifts into forever, only
breaking where the little streams and small
brooks bend. With compressed sounds.
Unheard yet echoing. And always there.

* NOMINATED FOR THE PUSHCART PRIZE, 2015

UPTURNED HAND

I see my upturned hand in the fog.
Familiar.
Yet distantly.
A hair's-breadth in reach I can almost
sense its tender protest
as the bones unfurl then draw close.
The same winged fingertips,
where the stirred shadows
pulse inside an outstretched palm,
laying peel like artful laceration.
A yellowed leaf falls to the ground,
and how my hand swiftly turns
upside down
in the smoky light,
tracing its gold edge,
leaving a marking of whispered skin.
When it grows dim, I stand still,
watching,
hand to be unfurled,
and pressed flat against my goose-
pimpled leg,
sensing a spilling breath
from within the marbled veins.

THE ELUSIVE MERMAID

Secrets in their tiny boxes, dreams sleep in glass,
occasionally you fish them out to swim among
the ordinary stones, hoping to catch a glance
of her floating hair and beryl-colored scaled
fins. Before sleep, you walk on coral reefs of
deep orange, emerging through murmuring
inlet where current is heavily stocked with fish.
Any moment the skies may darken and the sea
spews billows in great ascent, and through the
narrow slit of the mist she may rise, when the
open earth, rumbling air, and sheer stone walls
of spray collide. She may walk to shore, peeling
free the briny coat, flesh molds over bone, the
moon churns gold on her tresses. Then how will
you explain the way your thoughts slide beneath
the half-light and the ghosts of bird rasp your
voice in pained cackle—when the head knows
not what the heart speculates. You will need to
speak the language of the sea, of a midnight's
wail that breathes beneath the underbelly of the
words, one part air, the other part earth. And
maybe, just maybe, as her limbs morph back
under the waves, memory will carry the part of
speech where delicate shift in barometer will
remind her of your refrained whisper, and some-
where in the midst of liquid depths, the tracing
of your vanishing leaves itself on lime-rich shales.

DOPPELGANGER

Light spills from beneath the awning,
nets in a puddle of tattooed air as it
travels over her pale features. A face
grows in concentration. Follows by an
exhaling of tangled peals. Searching
for escape. Dizzy from the pull of swift
release and jarring hysteria, she unfurls
those long fingertips. Reaching for the
buoyant silhouette. Dovetailing with the
flutter of its yellow haired river. It nibbles
at the fingered suspension. Soft eyes, one
in a surprise caught, and the other veils
in shadow, leaning back into itself. Doubt
latches on to the skirt of the percussive
energy, sluggish. Like a naked dandelion
head floating awkwardly with broken stem,
empties through of downy plume. At the
sudden stir of air passing over them,
recognition shapes. In condensation and
smoke. Where the light is enchained and
acoustic vignettes tote along to shoulder
the notes of memory over. It knows what
she knows. It feels the same impressions
of her sensibility and riddled dreams. Atoms
dance across twined fingers. Breaths fusing
at the nubs in an ever curving flow of ions.
Twin bones. Twin fates. Forging into one.
Into an alphabet of matter and light.

A KNITTED DAY

One morning
I woke with the sun
wearing my face and I knitted
until all the dropped stitches
and the joining ends were no
more than pale specks in the light.
Perhaps I should have spun
sideways and turned on the
kerosene lantern that lay upon
the wardrobe bay when the
thick clouds curtained
the outside dim,
instead I let the night
crocheted my dainty feet,
patched tight the
fractured skin where the
thin bone of the needle
narrowed into wool,
then it wove the
gold moon in the
strands of my
French twist
as I trailed it
behind me
to sleep.

UNIVERSAL CARVING

The midnight train departed from Hampton Court station. He went on murmuring through the signaled horns. Held between a light-struck hooves of the air and shadowed carriage. And half-devoured under an English blasting rain. "It's quite docile actually for this time of year, darling", he said. I'd always known he liked the soggy cold, for his eyes were stained deep of teal-slate orbs. I snuck a glance towards the beyond sky. An infinite dark, peppered with hurrying trees and spray. At the sheer edge of horizon, the armored jaw of the wind was lopping off the moon about its neck with a fine cutlass, draining nearly the ashy gold. While the torrent swept wide its watery bone, plunging down the metal roof then gutting through the graveled earth. A liquid violence. Yet, nothing more than a mutual universal carving. Where the depths of chaos pillaged outside and soaring notes of passion caressed within. And never was there a more curious state than being caved inside an intimate skin of a lover and that of the cleaving pulses of rain.

GRAPHIC NOVEL

Now and again I traced the veins of those cold,
nameless things within me and wonder if I had
loved you too long. Blue marrows, turned darkly
blue with your eyes, bled glimpses of a graphic
novel we might have written.

So I sat and wrote about our marriage life untold:
empty pleas knelt cross-legged and became wise,
guilt lived among swift blood cells with secrets
trailed up the staircase then round the boudoir's
way, even the pale shade of teal on the wall spread
awkwardly against scores of vodka and gin and
pungent rose spanned across the hotel sheets.

As I was to paint you into linguistic calligraphy,
the sum of you teased then danced away with
eager legs devoid of details, your shapes, textures
and patterns, your scent on the pillows steeped in
nuances of another. Inside this house, all battles
between human and fate laid sleeping on our bed,
muffled moans and groans and I beside.

Perhaps I have edged too close to precipice where
there was nowhere to go but down, and if only my
waiting there could be met with words inside a smile
empty of metaphors, while I reached out, shaking
the partial play believing my hero would pour out
the pages.

CONSENT TO NOTHING, AND YOURSELF UNSEEING

Like long drinks from a tureen of a deep
lake, you gulp in bold liquid earth with
each sip a familiar sedative pregnant on
your tongue. You are thinking you come
here for convivial loneliness, where chaos
drops by once or twice for your friendly
ear and a few polite "how goes its jostle
at the elbow, but whether its habitués care
too little or not at all, you hope everyone
is alike in their ignorance and wretched-
ness. Of course how much strength for a
stranger to demand such from you when
they are no more than an afterthought is
a torque of poison, when you just long to
slip inside the fluid spill, becoming a speck
of foamed bubble staining on the beer glass,
lurking beyond nothing and sweet unseeing.
Vapid and sad and your last droplets con-
sumed, perhaps you should whistle at the
barkeep for another long drink, before your
hold on the night shrinks by the wayside,
and your stoic pride stretches so thick that
you no longer give a damn.

SYNCHRONICITY

I see him,
and the shadows fall back.
Everything pales behind where
his silhouette slopes on the
fresh-turned earth.
Taking hold of his coat's lapel,
the leathered skin feels grainy
between my fingertips,
like how his shaggy beard chafes
my breasts raw,
roaming over the pale chasm lay.
A curious sensation probes from
under the weight and erosion
of his sinew,
stretches itself into the linings of
my inner cells—
searching for traces of us
on the other side of synchronicity.
I swallow whole the distance, the sea,
the passing time,
the many hours on bitten tongues.
hungered words and labored ships.
Because somewhere in the depths
of memory,
there was a hiding place and in it,
my lover and I.

SMALL AND SMALLER

Inside her cupped hands
sprouts a small universe,
inside this universe,
another one lays smaller—
it is not a bird that takes root,
nor a mouse,
rather a sharp question
that presses its lips against moist skin,
where ink notes leak into alphabets,
incise through tiny beads of perspiration—
words churn this way and that,
but they could not know,
taking a turn back,
to which their clusters of deformity
would be the weight she would never regain—
instead,
now they lay soft and yielding,
and even if they were to step out of her hands,
the air would grab hold
of their whiskers-like-wings
and carry them towards the edge of the unknown—
so they will stagnate where
deep whimpering drifts by in the universe,
write up new letters as it has done before
when she opens
one hand and closes the other

RU

English is my day-to-day language that I barely understand. Vietnamese, the tongue of my mother's land, is the one in sleepwalking, I dream of home. It lets me put into spoken sounds of the old city's dampness and grime, cigarettes smoke warm through my father's accented syllables trailing his terrain of speech. I sit cross-legged at the bottom of the staircase, humming Ru, a quiet folk lullaby that my mother often sang me to sleep, its front-gate welcoming, moon-lit courtyard trickles earthward inserted words "au a o", which are a bit tricky for a foreign tongue to emulate. Somewhere in the foyer, a handmade paper lamp rouses to waking beams of gold, turns bright my breaths which are a million rustic wisps born from flour and rice grains, where water buffaloes still tromp the dense paddy fields. Out where the fish pond, lemon grass thistle and root lotus spill entrails into the water, more pink than green, more flowers than leaves. I surrender my voice to the breeze knowing it would land on the lisle, like a minstrel who's set aside the old way of storytelling with ink and quill, instead, I pour my words into a sonant river straying across soft tongue and hard teeth, echoing the homage of jasmine tea percolating over porcelain china cup, topped with fluid ricochets of the Mekong riverboat's paddle wheels cutting through the waning gas light. But like a theater host shushing her enthusiastic audience at the final curtain calls, I emerge behind the veil of dark, discovering the stage is empty and the play needs to be rewritten, over and over. "Hello", calls a familiar voice from the other side of morning fog, "home is space between every letter, home is sounds between silence, so someday, maybe you'll come back to visit." My voice releases into its voice box, my silhouette holds a cauldron of understanding, simmers in history.

THERE IS A CRACK IN EVERYTHING

I carried my pocket watch to remind me of
winter, when the ducks flew south and fish
glided down the iced bottom lake, even host
of pansy bowed quietly away as I turned up
the collar to ward off December raw—

a duffel bag on one arm, I righted it over the
shoulder, cobalt eyes took in the lofty blue
masonry walls on my left and quietly moved
up the brick body, even at this late hour with
poor lighting, I can still make out the girl's
silhouette at the second story window, yellow
hair gathered at the nape, dimness drunk her
whole—

she sat with her side profile partially hidden
in shadows, at odd moments, she reached out
to touch her hand on the glass bay, as if to
kindle the air into warmth with the staying of
her flesh, the window frosted up when she
pulled back those pale fingertips, and the form
of such arcs was a marvel to witness, like a
painter with her master strokes that drew me
back into a whorl where all things born from
the universe—

I watched and spiraled into her pull as the sky
spent its fury about me, cold breaths snapped
to the snow's quick tug when nocturnal ghosts
sailed over my face, there I stood, leaving traces
on the frozen earth, sharing intimacy with a girl
whose catatonic imprint left cracks in everything,
yet I knew that salvation would require so little
beyond this illusion of warmth—

THE LEAVING GIRL

nature not thoughts that stir her,
most times conscious, sometimes defiant,
it is strange to think of language,
space and time as threefold immersions of who she is
underneath her curiosity:
the quiet hours teeming on the changing seasons,
the waterlogged hyphens and half-way question marks,
the discharge of music through her fingertips
is a scattered shot of shavings
flapping wings and flying away—

she used to believe she could climb up straight
over the spine of her hiding place,
where thoughts flare in rings of dim violets,
and lullabies kneed the marsh of her sinews into sleep,
but instead,
when her brain begins to fret,
she creeps around the curves and sere troughs,
her hands move with hunched fingers
clutching the wisps of decades gone,
her feet:
fixed in carbon and clay,
lurch forward like a beetle on its graphite trail,
tracking veins of sediments as coarse-grained and indelicate
as a girl's leaving—

MIGRAINE

My migraine presents itself as an old woman, with heavily wrinkled face, traveling in a taxi. Fever of a century and a half old settles on her eyelids, jockeys over the haggard face. Handkerchief white as the snowflakes peeking out from her deep dress' pocket, soaks in crusty flesh. With the wind snakes through the half-rolled window and the sun a brilliant stream of gold, prickly thoughts spill across the left temple. Leaving scribbles in stark spool of light. When the wheels pull to a stop at the curb, she lets the words trickle down the wet sidewalk. Drain away into a strung elegy of incoherence. Its supple spine caresses the end of her linen on the way down, spilling of pity and sulfur air. Wagging its autumn tail on the skirt of her bent torso, a silenced nerve center of ghosts. Turning from voices and echoes she rarely infers that are flecked with ill-mercy, she scours with alarm the spewing clumsiness on spent legs. Held on ambiguous sensations of conflicting senses and scenery. Hunting down release. Hunting for vacancy. Suspends between sky and dust. And she, a speck of grain dangling on the theft of wit. Limbs numbed and dragging, cradling madness in her bone.

THE CASUALTY OF A FORGOTTEN BOOK

the words come
barreling out of a book,
slightly
round in shape,
yet sharp and angled
at the flutter of fingertips—
a quick drip of "and"s,
then a torrent
of "dust"s
tumble into my hand—
so I lay their broken bones
like a wrong symphony,
flat on my palm,
they appear crisp-skinned
with veins of toasted brown—
a concerted sigh,
I gather them into
a pile of alphabet
grief

LINGUISTICS SILENCE

He began as we pressed close,
the two of us,
huddling within the
rotating peals of syllables
and nuances.
The twin whips of genteel verse
and obscene language by two
exhaustive geniuses:
neither an amateur,
bruised the air,
leaving deep impressions upon its
wafer-thin skin.
When darkness comes,
in soft caress
he declares,
a seduction,
for I would hear
the whispered words travel with stones,
regurgitating the spawning wisdom
from the conjugal hole they'd wiggled through.
And perhaps a sonant or two
will shift it into something
altogether else,
darker even,
like a betrayed kiss
while delicate as a butterfly-leafing
of a winged hand upon skin, quietly
stirs in its metamorphic tongue.

TIME

Within an ever ebbing sense of time,
you stood in a forgotten place,
but never a forgotten thought.
The time before now and the time before that,
you had lived in poor pockets of void:
slept under torn tapestry of sky,
dined on meager bowls of dirt
scooped out the dregs of life
with a plastic spoon;
tumbling, weaving, panting, drowning
at no time to have been absolutely sure
that life from which wrinkles are born,
shall lend you mercy in this vain enterprise.
You have spared no mind to the ilk of pride,
you have grown as a pauper, no smaller than a mite
held fixed in doubt, clad thin by the pinches of salt
and lost lullabies.
Always strayed far from the world's pearly gate,
never a guest at its cozy dinners or fancy balls.
But, the person you were and the person you are:
the half-lost and half-whole
the half-woke and half-dreaming,
doubled over with hunger when it
spawned and gnawed into your belly
like an infected cancer.
So you slackened your legs, spilled your virtues
and gave yourself leave to
throttle life and drink from its gilded spout.
Your eyes shut tight, your mouth unfurled
whose lips swigged clean all the bitter poison
and honeyed wine.

A FACE IN AN ENDLESS SEA

Into the waking sea of stirring succubi,
I walk through the cobblestone with
measured insolence. It is my life and
yet it is not. It is a known street yet
serpents edge the ground my feet have
not trodden upon. A revised life. While
it is endured on a rewritten script. Like
curious pages from an aged notebook,
flush of spell-casting recipes and archaic
theorems. Drafted in inked calligraphy
from my hand held within someone else's.
I am thinking I ought to shake away the
cold fingertips that I cannot slake. And
what it would be like to will my private
thoughts, and travel without fragmented
memories. But my verbal bones are deep-
seated and buried, pack together to guard
the centermost. Leaving bare the external
skin. To which I persist on as a compressed
infection, neither growing smaller in mass
nor vanishing into a fictional poem. Yet,
I know not with certainty whether I am
the vast sky or its dispersed molecules.
Or just a face in an endless sea.

INVISIBILITY IN WATER

A leaf floating towards you through slate dense water granulated by the morning's shadows. Last breaths of the soon vanishing wade in wisps of iridescence, from the tall eaves of horsetail reeds to the flat spine of river moss, where ghost of faces echoes back in sprigs.

There, you kneel just behind fine contours of the breeze, so the trail of light lurches about in abandoning, bleaching things of rust and the liquid world to a soft glow, in place of you. Then your hand dips into water, though it makes no sound, but how will you explain your orphaned fingers combing the ripples as dregs of sunlight sneak away under vestibules of dreaming, with knuckles cold beneath dark's inquisition.

Watching your flesh get torn into a speckled mosaic by the fractal smattering of water, you are frightened your feet would fail, and your eyes would weep, when you'd wake to a lost innocence, to be simultaneously right in front of yourself yet just shy of invisibility is like springing up from a long winter's nap without the sweet promise of spring, and not unlike that to a little death, yours is a morose slumbering borne inside some liquid melancholia.

A three-time Pushcart Prize nominee, Lana Bella is an author of two chapbooks, *Under My Dark* (Crisis Chronicles Press, 2016) and *Adagio* (Finishing Line Press, forthcoming), has had poetry and fiction featured with over 300 journals, *2River, California Quarterly, Chiron Review, Columbia Journal, Otoliths, Poetry Salzburg Review, San Pedro River Review, The Hamilton Stone Review, The Ilanot Review, The Writing Disorder, Third Wednesday,* and *Tipton Poetry Journal,* among others. She resides in the US and the coastal town of Nha Trang, Vietnam, where she is a mom of two far-too-clever-frolicsome imps.

https://www.facebook.com/Lana-Bella-789916711141831/

www.ingramcontent.com/pod-product-compliance
Lightning Source LLC
LaVergne TN
LVHW041515070426
835507LV00012B/1578